ALFRED's SACRED PERFORMER COLLECTIONS

Late Intermediate Piano

What Can I Play
Book 4: July & August Services

Arranged by Cindy Berry

10 Easily Prepared Piano Arrangements for July & August Services

Have you ever thought, "I wish I had *one* piano book that included appropriate hymn arrangements for the next couple of months"? As a church accompanist, I have shared that thought with you! *What Can I Play on Sunday?* is a series of six books, each book containing easily prepared pieces that are appropriate for a two-month period of the year. Book 1 is for January and February, Book 2 for March and April, and so on. Each book serves as a wonderful resource for your worship-planning needs for each season of the year. If your church uses Lectionary-based worship, these arrangements should be appropriate for those needs as well.

Book 4 contains arrangements that are appropriate for the months of July and August, and includes patriotic selections for the Fourth of July, as well as many timeless, favorite hymns. The other books in this series are as follows:

Book 1: January and February
Book 2: March and April
Book 3: May and June
Book 5: September and October
Book 6: November and December

I pray that you will find this series useful as you play your praises to God on Sundays, or use these arrangements for your own personal worship times.

Cindy Berry

AMERICA THE BEAUTIFUL (FOURTH OF JULY) 2
AMERICA (MY COUNTRY, 'TIS OF THEE) (FOURTH OF JULY) 5
COME, YE SINNERS, POOR AND NEEDY (GENERAL) 8
BRETHREN, WE HAVE MET TO WORSHIP (GENERAL) 12
O WORD OF GOD INCARNATE (GENERAL) 16
WE ARE CLIMBING JACOB'S LADDER (GENERAL) 20
HOLY GOD, WE PRAISE THY NAME (GENERAL) 24
GOD WILL TAKE CARE OF YOU (GENERAL) 28
ALL HAIL THE POWER OF JESUS' NAME (GENERAL) 32
WHERE HE LEADS ME (GENERAL) 37

Copyright © MMVI by Alfred Publishing Co., Inc.
All rights reserved. Printed in USA.
ISBN-10: 0-7390-4759-0
ISBN-13: 978-0-7390-4759-0

America the Beautiful

Samuel A. Ward
Arr. Cindy Berry

America
(My Country, 'Tis of Thee)

Traditional
Arr. Cindy Berry

With confidence (♩ = ca. 96)

Come, Ye Sinners, Poor and Needy

William Waller
Arr. Cindy Berry

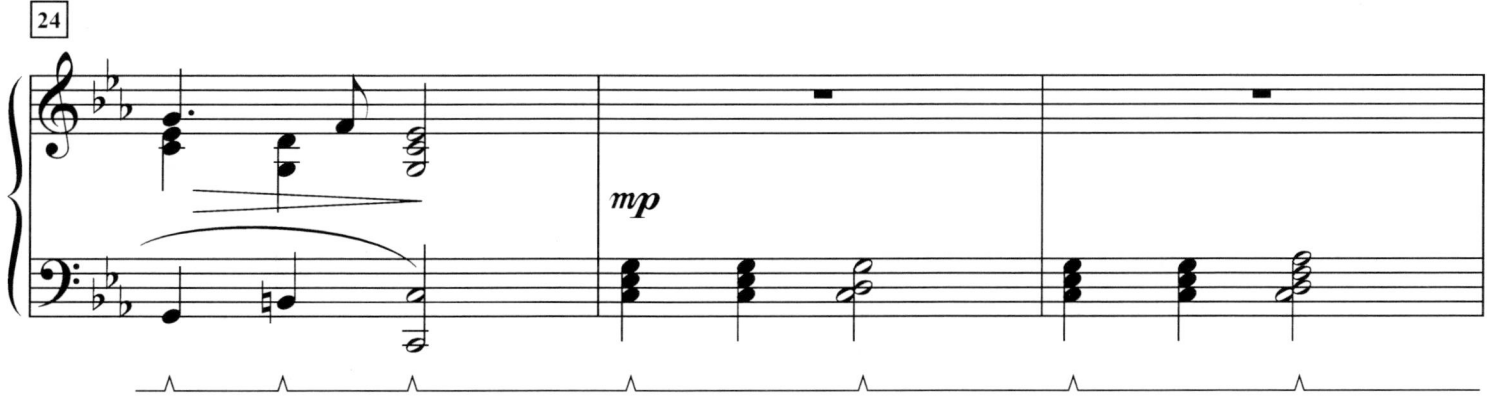

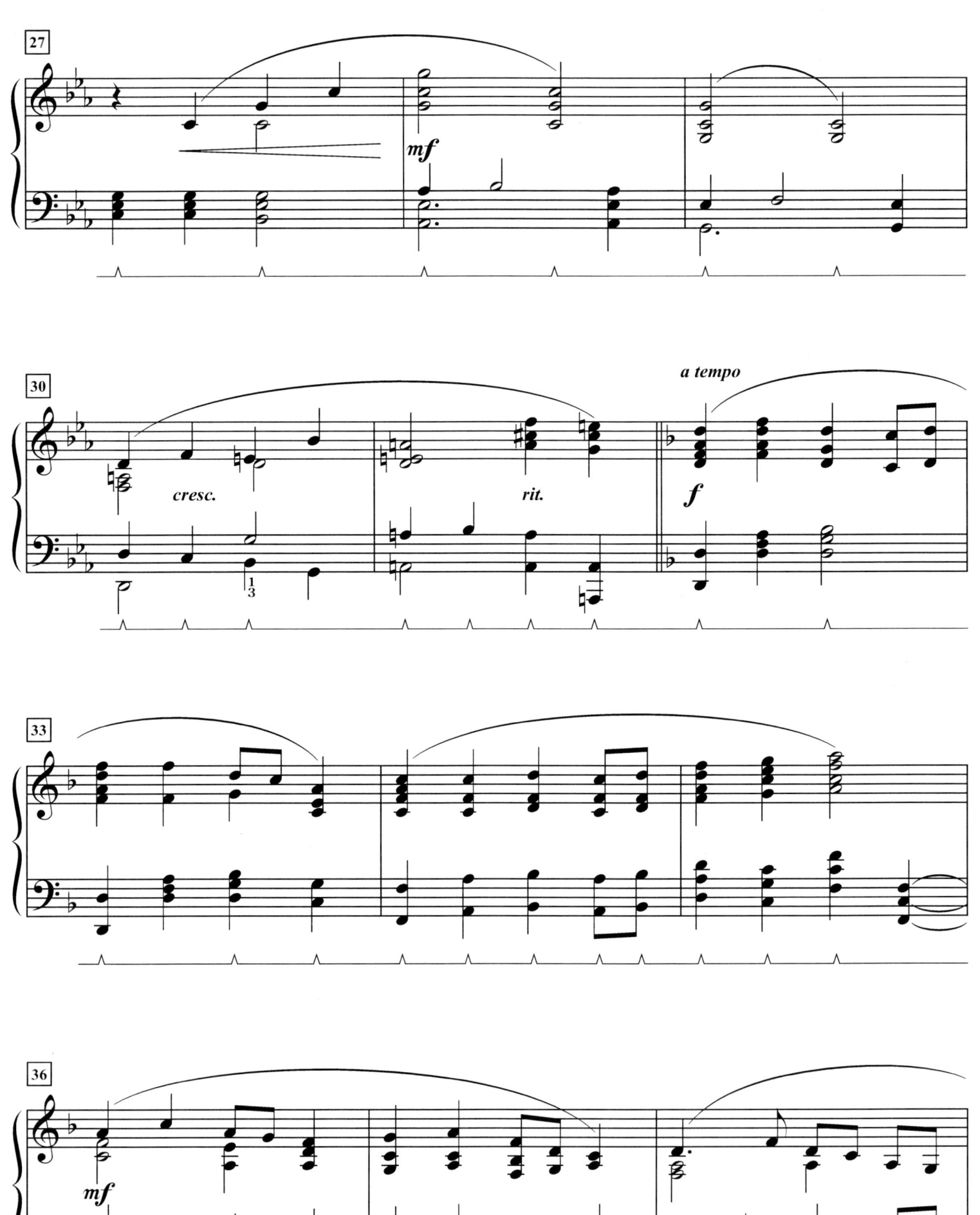

Brethren, We Have Met to Worship

William Moore
Arr. Cindy Berry

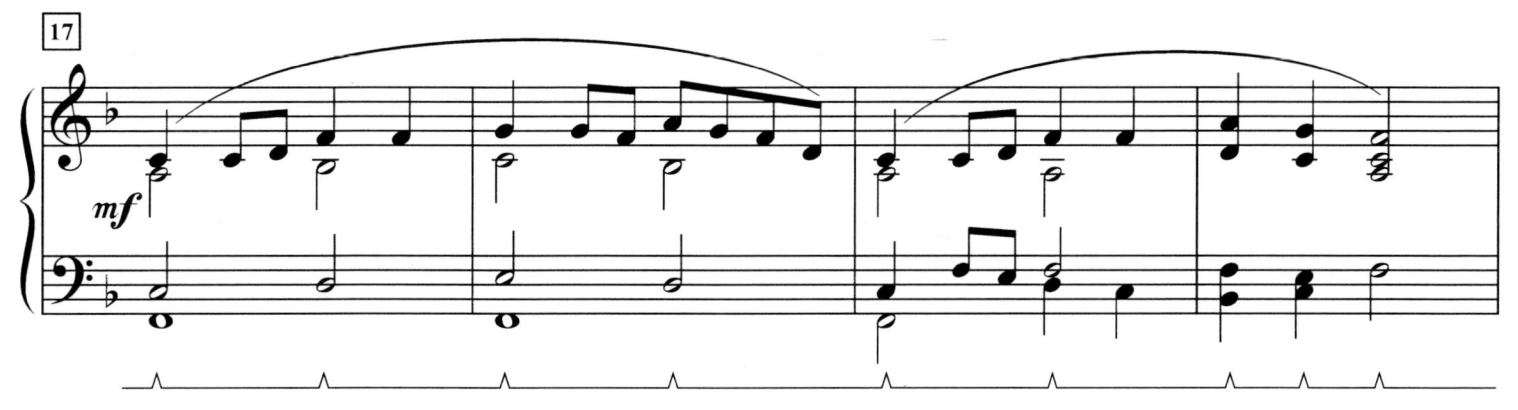

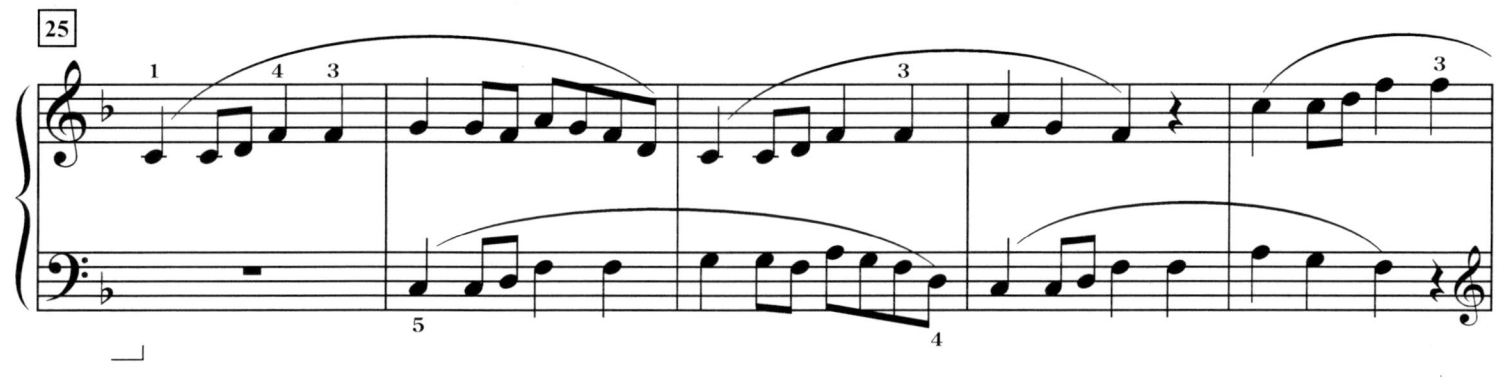
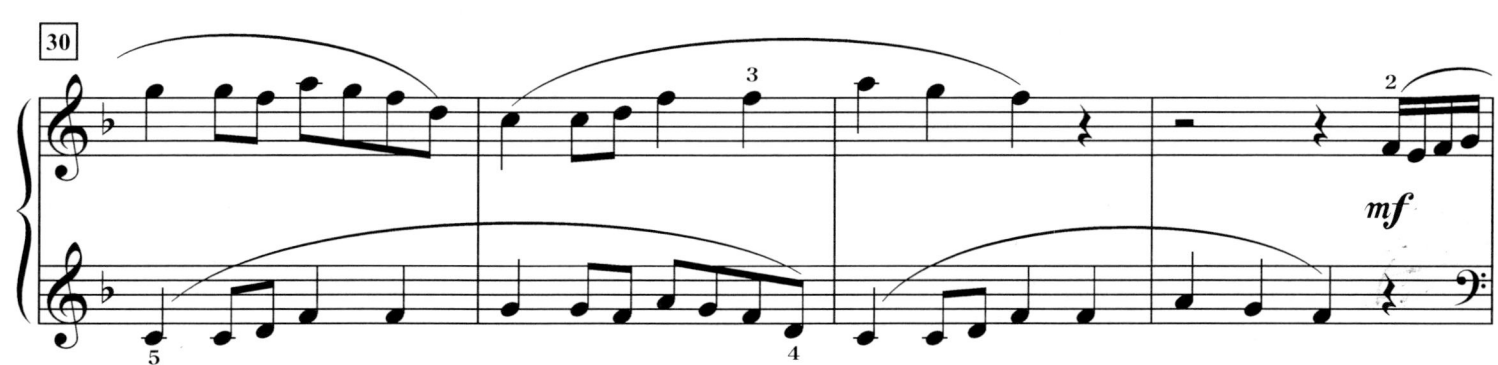

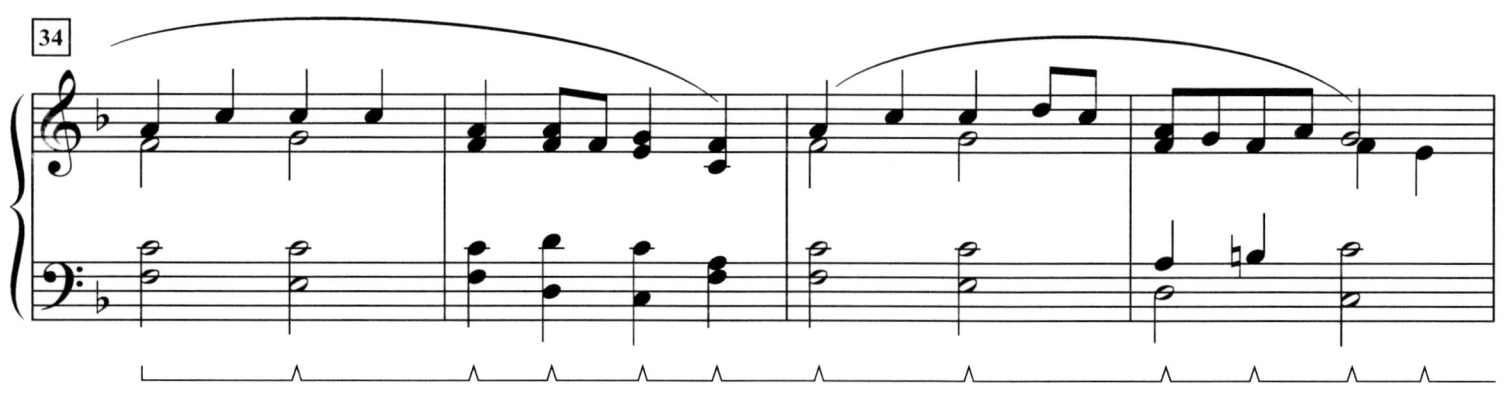

O Word of God Incarnate

Neuvermehrtes Gesangbuch
Meiningens, 1693
Arr. Cindy Berry

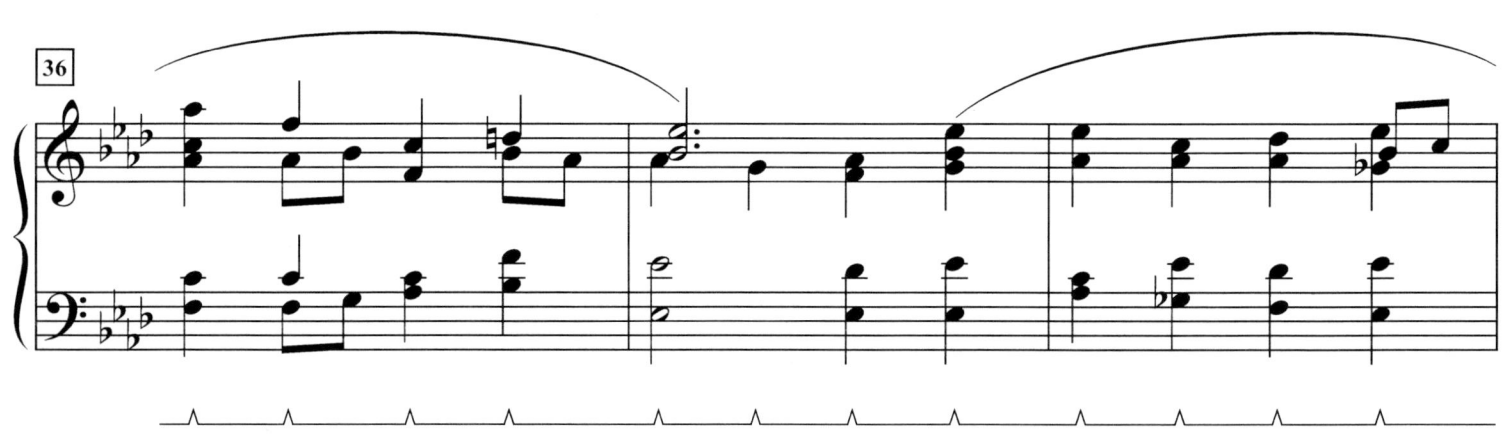

We Are Climbing Jacob's Ladder

Spiritual
Arr. Cindy Berry

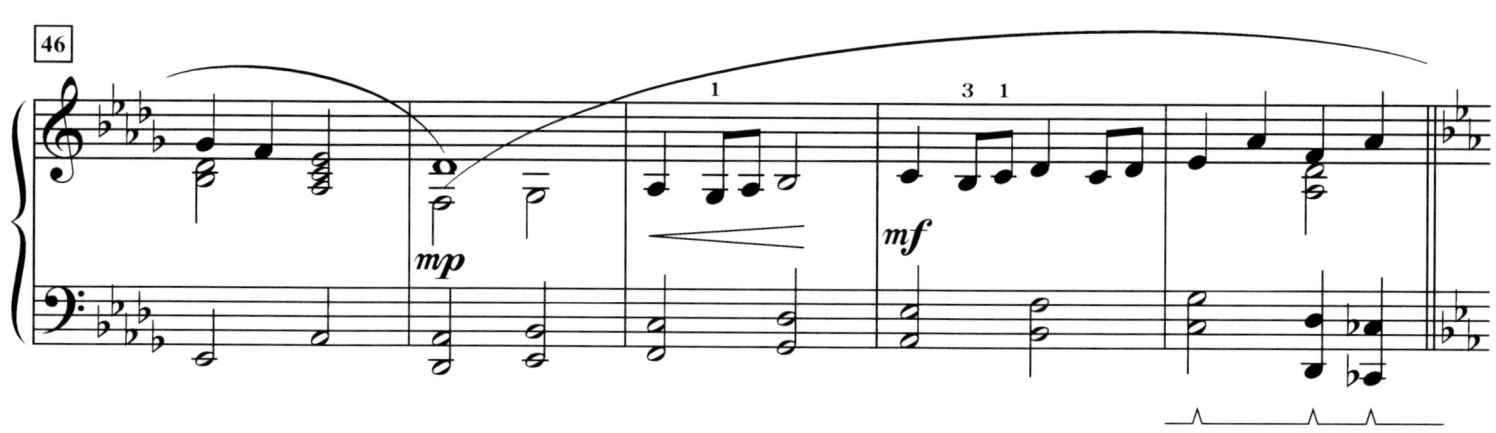

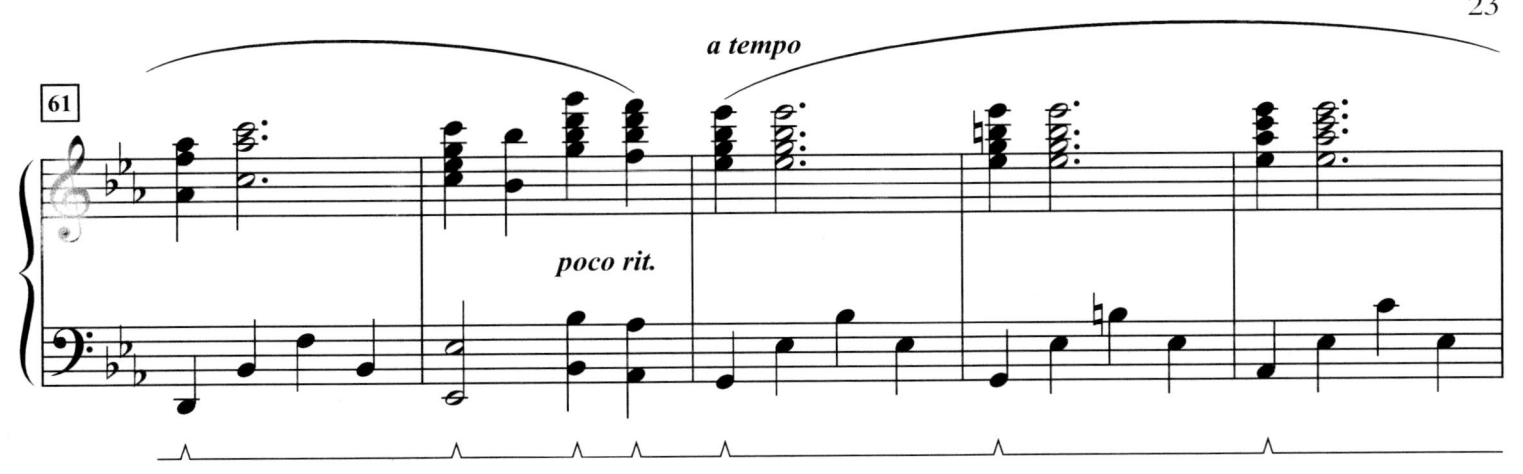
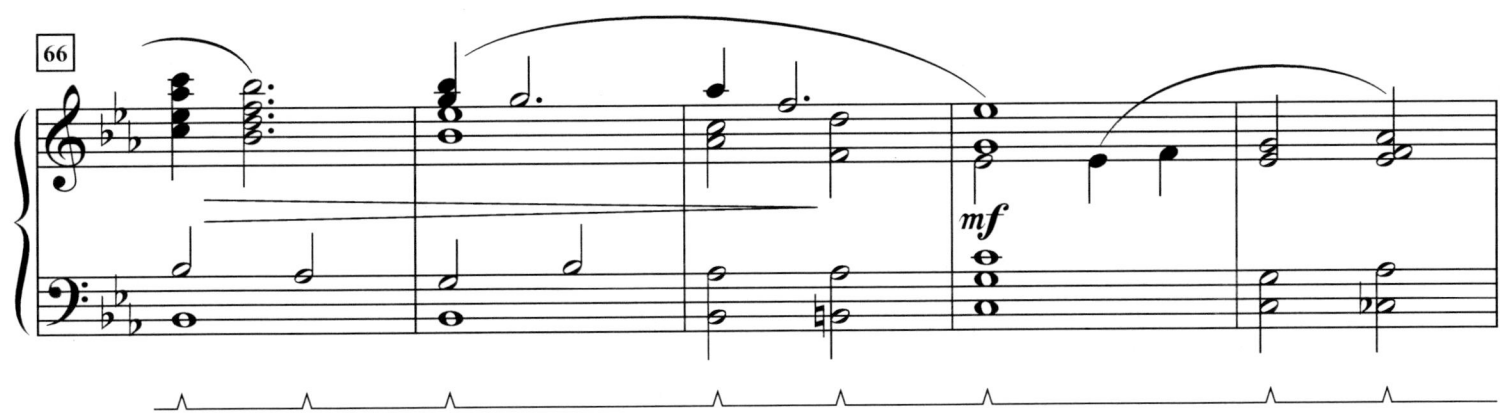
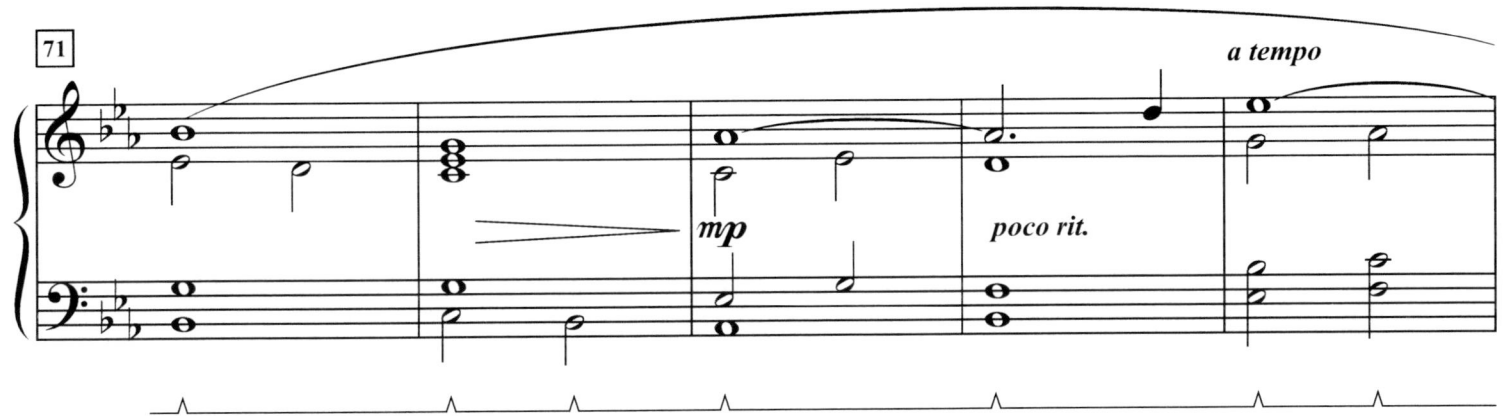
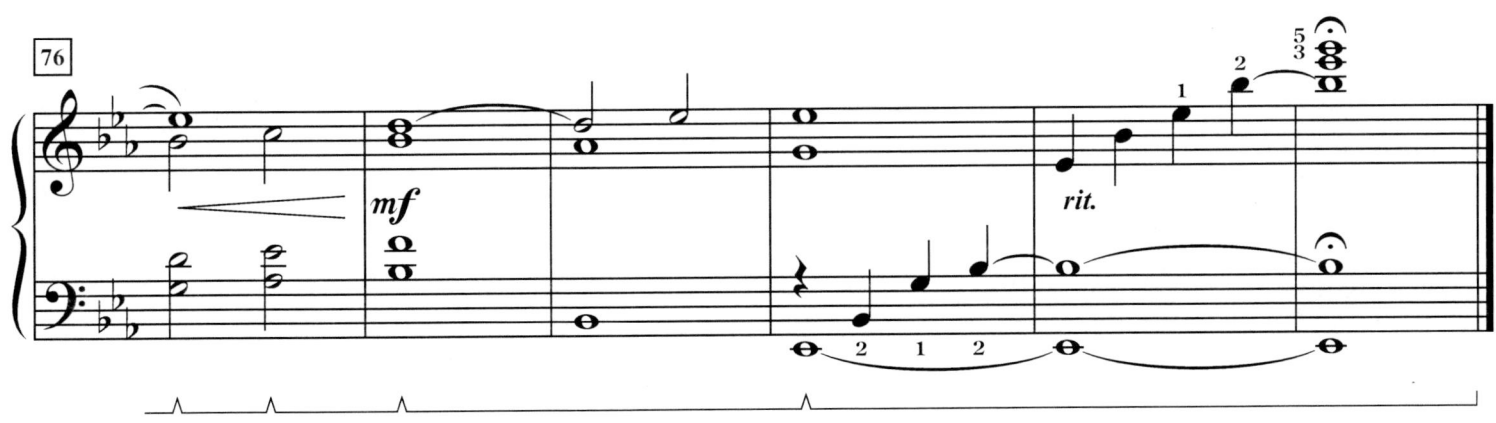

Holy God, We Praise Thy Name

Katholisches Gesangbuch
Vienna, ca. 1774
Arr. Cindy Berry

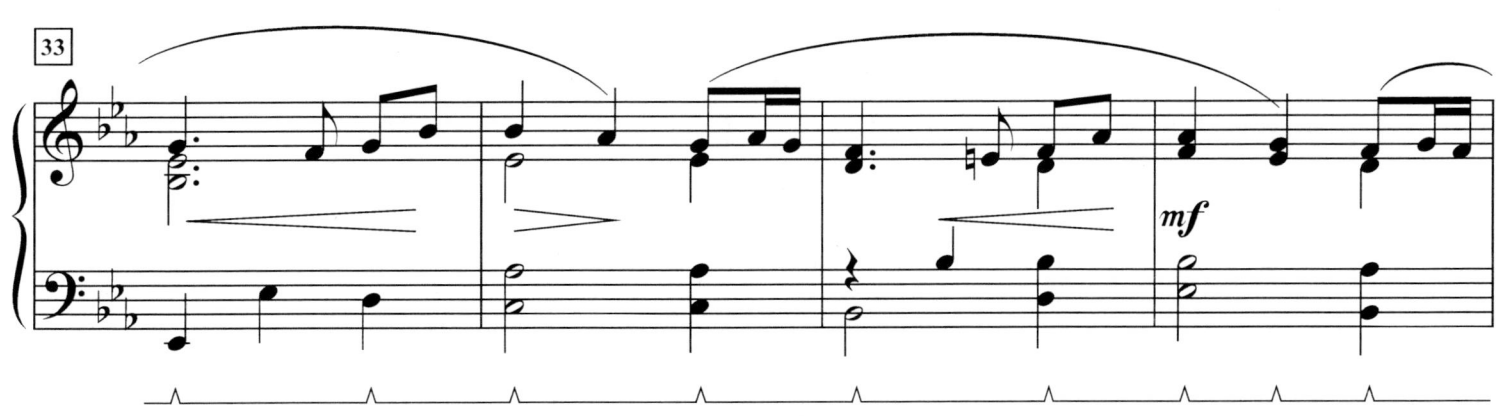

God Will Take Care of You

Walter S. Martin
Arr. Cindy Berry

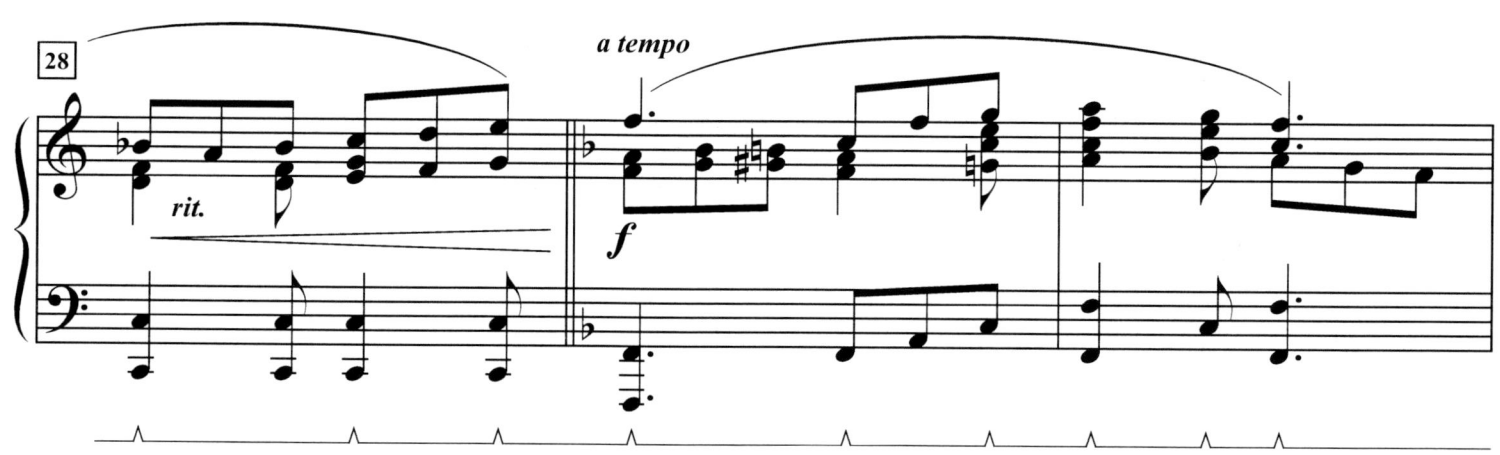

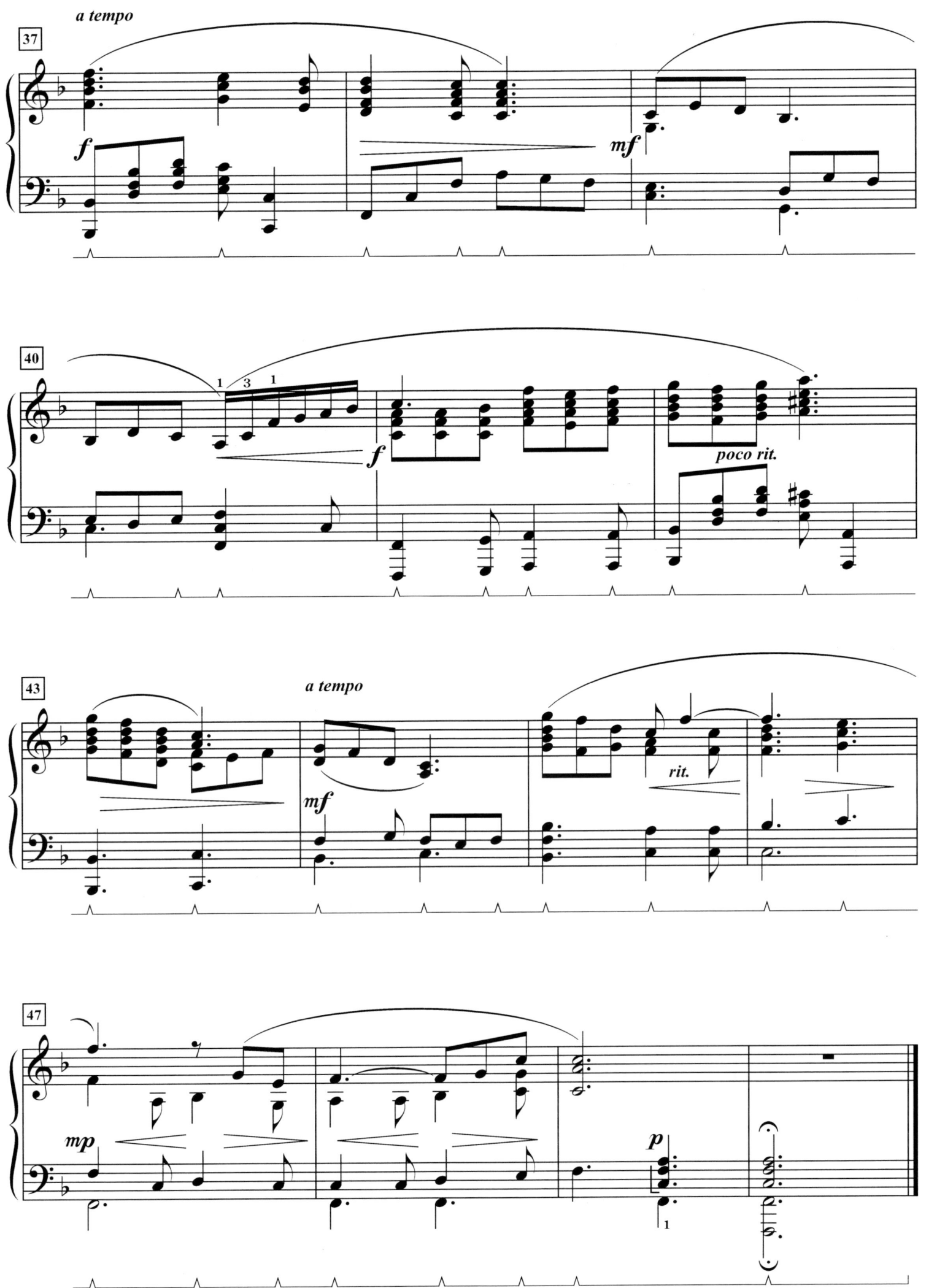

All Hail the Power of Jesus' Name

Oliver Holden
Arr. Cindy Berry

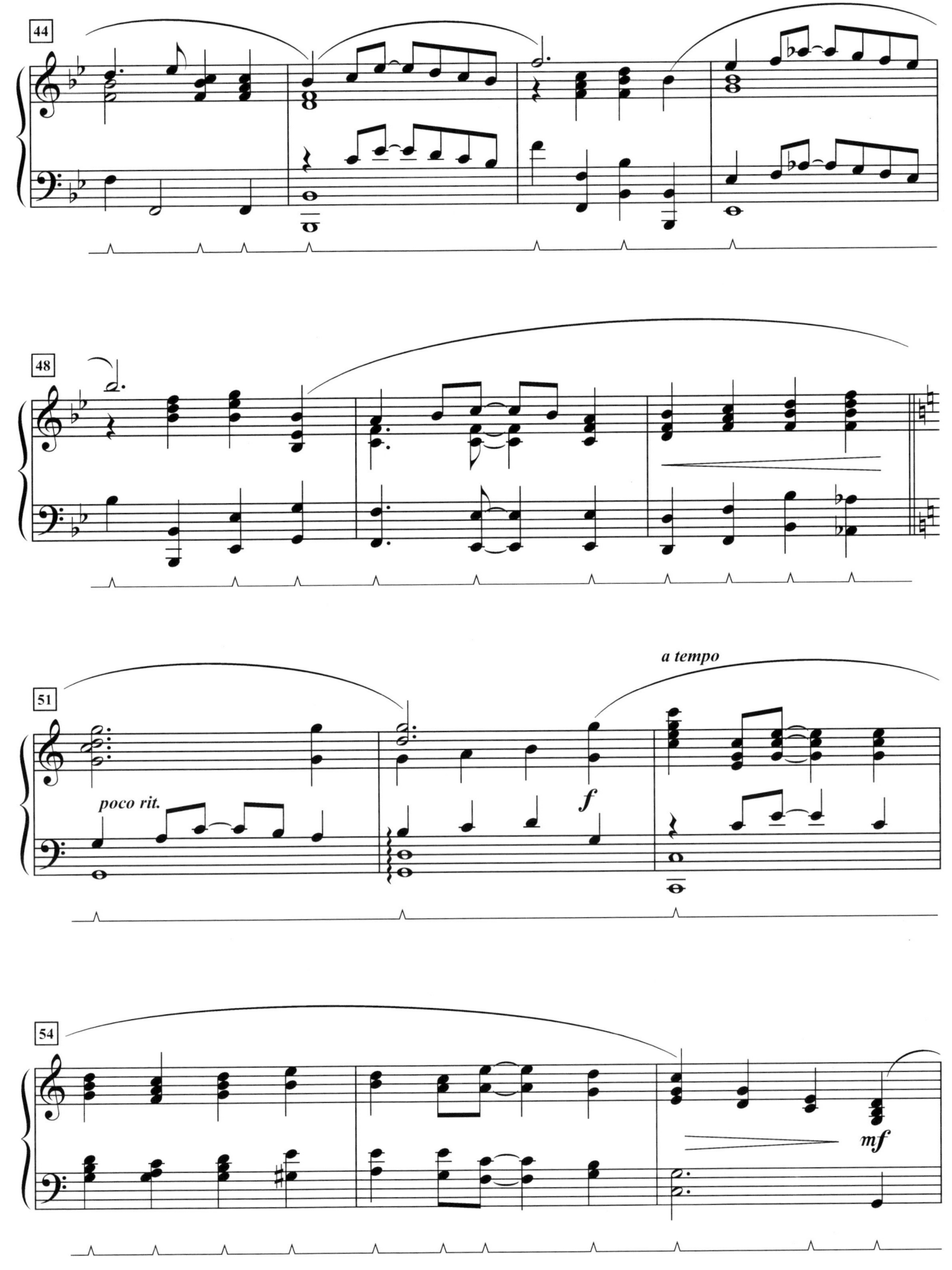

Where He Leads Me

John S. Norris
Arr. Cindy Berry

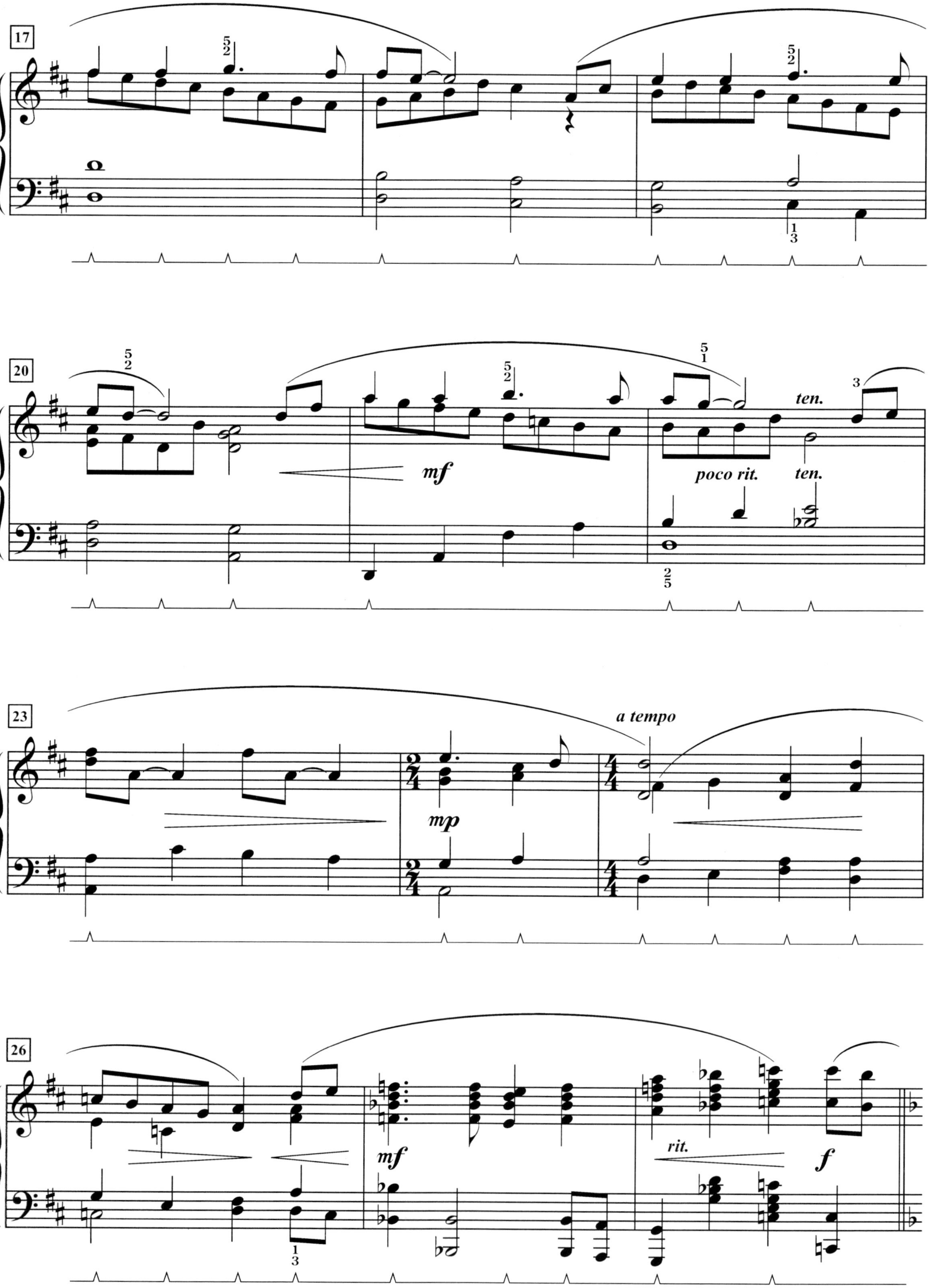
17
20
mf
poco rit.
ten.
ten.
23
a tempo
mp
26
mf
rit.
f